Carol Burniston
Color-Splashed
QUILTS

FUSE FUN APPLIQUÉ TO YOUR PIECING

C&T PUBLISHING

Text copyright © 2007 by Carol Burniston

Artwork copyright © 2007 by C&T Publishing, Inc.

Publisher: AMY MARSON

Editorial Director: GAILEN RUNGE

Acquisitions Editor: JAN GRIGSBY

Editors: ANGEL HAWTHORNE & KESEL WILSON

Technical Editors: CAROLYN AUNE & ELIN THOMAS

Copyeditor/Proofreader: WORDFIRM INC.

Cover Designer: KRISTEN YENCHE

Book Designer: ROSE SHEIFER-WRIGHT

Production Coordinator: TIM MANIBUSAN

Illustrator: KIRSTIE L. PETTERSEN

Photography by C&T Publishing, Inc., unless otherwise noted

Published by C&T Publishing, Inc., P.O. Box 1456, Lafayette, CA 94549

Library of Congress Cataloging-in-Publication Data

Burniston, Carol,

Color-splashed quilts : fuse fun appliqué to your piecing / Carol Burniston.

p. cm.

ISBN-13: 978-1-57120-441-7 (paper trade : alk. paper)

ISBN-10: 1-57120-441-5 (paper trade : alk. paper)

1. Appliqué--Patterns. 2. Patchwork--Patterns. I. Title.

TT779.B7745 2007

746.44'5041--dc222007008554

Printed in China

10 9 8 7 6 5 4 3 2 1

Acknowledgments

I would like to acknowledge my wonderful family. They have filled my life with adventure and joy. Sometimes I could have lived without the adventure, but, hey, that's what families are for.

Dedication

This book is dedicated to my husband, Jack Burniston. Twenty-nine and a half years ago, he was patrolling the freeways of southern California as a highway patrolman. One night he pulled into an all-night diner where I was working to pay my way through college. Jack asked me out, but I said no. He came back the next night and asked me out again. I answered maybe. He came back the third night to ask me out, and this time I said okay. Soon after that, I said "I do." Almost thirty years and three kids later, I'm glad he was persistent!

Contents

Introduction

Greetings!

The quilt designs in this book were inspired by what I like to think of as the simple delights of life—wiggly puppies, ice skates, fresh fruit and fragrant flowers, adventure stories of far-off places, kaleidoscopes, and small, cute creatures.

At heart I'm a simple person. It doesn't take much to keep me happy—a clean sewing room with a cleared-off cutting table, a stack of new fabrics, and an idea for a new quilt!

One day last summer when I had planned to spend an afternoon working on a new quilt, the phone rang. It was my sister Barbara calling to ask whether I'd like to join her kayaking on nearby Whiskeytown Lake here in California. Although I had only gone kayaking once before, it sounded fun. Kayaks move and turn easily, and paddling on the lake is relaxing. "Inspiration for my new quilt!" I rationalized and headed out.

It was wonderful maneuvering our kayaks around that lazy, warm summer afternoon. Surrounded by the beauty of nature, I was reminded once again that it's the simple wonders of life that I love so much.

My hope is that the whimsical quilt designs in this book—filled with fun, bright colors and easy-to-follow instructions—will be delightfully simple for you and simply delightful to make.

Carol Burniston

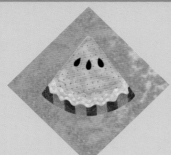

Summer Fruit

Designed and made by Carol Burniston.
Machine quilted by Janet Murdock.
Finished quilt: 63˝ × 72˝
Finished blocks: 9˝ × 9˝

This quilt represents the best of summertime: long, hot days with refreshing watermelon slices, strawberries served with whipped cream, and peach ice cream. Stitch this tantalizing quilt and capture the flavor of summer.

Materials You'll Need

- 4 yards yellow batik print for appliquéd blocks and border strips
- 1 yard blue batik print 1 for border strips
- ⅝ yard blue batik print 2 for binding
- 4¼ yards fabric for backing
- 71″ × 80″ piece of batting
- 5¾ yards lightweight 22″-wide fusible web
- Monofilament thread
- Template plastic (optional)

For triangle appliqués

- 1¾ yards total assorted blue batik prints

For peach appliqués

- ¼ yard dark orange print
- ¼ yard medium orange print
- ⅛ yard brown print

For strawberry appliqués

- ¼ yard red print
- ⅛ yard green print

For pear appliqués

- ¼ yard medium green print
- Scraps of light green and brown prints

For watermelon appliqués

- ¼ yard pink print
- ⅛ yard light green print
- ⅛ yard dark green print
- Scraps of black print

For grape appliqués

- Scrap of green print
- ⅛ yard dark purple
- ⅛ yard each of 2 different medium purple prints

Cutting the Fabric

Cut strips from the crosswise grain of the fabric.

From the yellow batik print, cut:

- 8 strips, 9½″ × 40″; crosscut into:
  30 squares, 9½″ × 9½″ (fruit foundation blocks)
- 6 strips, 5″ × 40″; crosscut into:
  22 rectangles, 5″ × 9½″ (outer foundation blocks)
  4 squares, 5″ × 5″ (corner foundation blocks)
- 1 strip, 1½″ × 40″; crosscut into:
  2 strips, 1½″ × 15″ (border)
- 12 strips, 1½″ × 40″

From the blue batik print 1, cut:

- 13 strips, 1½″ × 40″ (border)
- 1 strip, 1½″ × 40″; crosscut into:
  2 strips, 1½″ × 15″ (border)
- 7 strips, 1″ × 40″ (border)
- 1 strip, 1″ × 40″; crosscut into:
  1 strip, 1″ × 15″ (border)

From the blue batik print 2, cut:

- 8 strips, 2½″ × 40″ (binding)

Cutting for Appliqué

The patterns for these appliqués are on pages 9–10. Refer to *Making Templates* (page 43).

For the fruit blocks, use:

- Pattern 1A: make 168 from the assorted blue batik prints.

For the Peaches, use:

- Pattern 1B: make 6 from the dark orange print.
- Pattern 1C: make 6 from the medium orange print.
- Pattern 1D: make 6 from the brown print.

For the Strawberries, use:

- Pattern 1E: make 6 from the red print.
- Pattern 1F: make 6 from the green print.

For the Pears, use:

- Pattern 1G: make 6 from the medium green print.
- Pattern 1H: make 6 from the light green print.
- Pattern 1I: make 6 from the brown print.

For the Watermelons, use:

- Pattern 1J: make 6 from the pink print.
- Pattern 1K: make 6 from the light green print.
- Pattern 1L: make 6 from the dark green print.
- Pattern 1M: make 18 from the black print.

For the Grapes, use:

- Pattern 1N: make 6 from the green print.
- Pattern 1O: make 84 from the dark purple.
- Pattern 1O: make 30 from each medium purple print (60 total).

Appliquéing the Blocks

You will need 56 appliquéd blocks: 30 fruit blocks (6 each of the Peach, Strawberry, Pear, Watermelon, and Grape blocks), 22 outer blocks, and 4 corner blocks. Refer to *Fusible Appliqué* (page 44).

1. For the fruit blocks, position and fuse 4 blue 1A triangles to each yellow batik 9½″ × 9½″ foundation square. Place the shortest edge of each 1A triangle ¼″ from each edge of the square, as shown. Make 30.

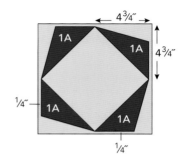

2. For the outer blocks, position and fuse 2 blue 1A triangles to each yellow batik 5″ × 9½″ foundation rectangle. Make 22.

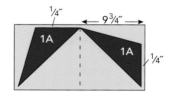

3. For the corner blocks, position and fuse 1 blue 1A triangle to each yellow batik 5″ × 5″ foundation square. Make 4.

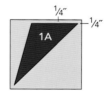

4. For the Peach blocks, use 6 squares from Step 1 for the foundations. Position and fuse peach parts 1B, 1C, and 1D. Make 6.

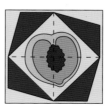

5. For the Strawberry blocks, use 6 squares from Step 1 for the foundations. Position and fuse strawberry parts 1E and 1F. Make 6.

6. For the Pear blocks, use 6 squares from Step 1 for the foundations. Position and fuse pear parts 1G, 1H, and 1I. Make 6.

7. For the Watermelon blocks, use 6 squares from Step 1 for the foundations. Position and fuse watermelon parts 1J, 1K, 1L, and 1M. Make 6.

8. For the Grape blocks, use 6 squares from Step 1 for the foundations. Position and fuse 1 green 1N stem and 14 dark purple grapes (10). Make 6.

9. Position and fuse 10 medium purple grapes (10) on top of the already fused dark purple part. Make 6.

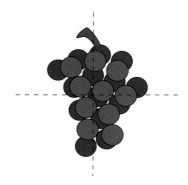

10. Finish the edges of the appliqués with a machine blanket stitch and monofilament thread.

Assembling the Quilt

Referring to the quilt photo (page 4) and the quilt assembly diagram (page 8), lay out the appliquéd blocks in 8 horizontal rows. Sew the blocks into rows. Press the seams in opposite directions. Sew the rows together. Press the seams in one direction.

Adding the Border

1. Sew the 13 blue 1½″ × 40″ strips end-to-end as needed and cut into eight 1½″ × 63½″ strips.

2. Sew the 7 blue 1″ × 40″ strips end-to-end as needed and cut into four 1″ × 63½″ strips.

3. Sew the 12 yellow 1½″ × 40″ strips end-to-end as needed and cut into four 1½″ × 63½″ strips and four 1½″ × 54½″ strips.

4. For the side borders, sew together 2 blue 1½″ × 63½″ strips, 2 yellow 1½″ × 63½″ strips, and 1 blue 1″ × 63½″ strip in the order shown. Press the seams toward the blue strips. Make 2.

5. For the border corners, sew together 2 blue 1½″ × 15″ strips, 2 yellow 1½″ × 15″ strips, and 1 blue 1″ × 15″ strip in the order shown. Press the seams toward the blue strips; then crosscut into 8 units 1½″ × 5″.

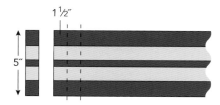

6. Sew one 1½″ × 5″ unit from Step 5 to each end of a 1½″ × 54½″ yellow strip from Step 3. Each yellow strip unit should now measure 1½″ × 63½″. Make 4.

7. For the top and bottom borders, sew together 2 blue 1½″ × 63½″ strips, 2 yellow 1½″ × 63½″ strip units from Step 6, and 1 blue 1″ × 63½″ strip in the order shown. Press the seams toward the blue strips. Make 2.

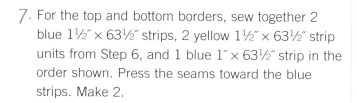

8. Sew the side borders to the quilt. Press the seams toward the borders. Sew the top and bottom borders to the quilt. Press the seams toward the borders.

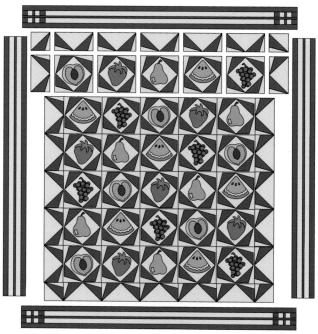

Quilt assembly diagram

Quilting and Binding

Refer to *Basic Quiltmaking Tips* (pages 43–47) as needed to finish your quilt.

Divide the backing fabric in half selvage-to-selvage. Re-seam and trim to make a 71″ × 80″ backing. Layer the quilt top, batting, and backing. Baste the three layers and quilt as desired. Make the binding using the 2½″-wide blue batik print 2 strips and finish the edges of the quilt.

Appliqué Patterns

The appliqué patterns are reversed for fusible appliqué. For hand appliqué, reverse the patterns and make templates (see *Making Templates*, page 43).

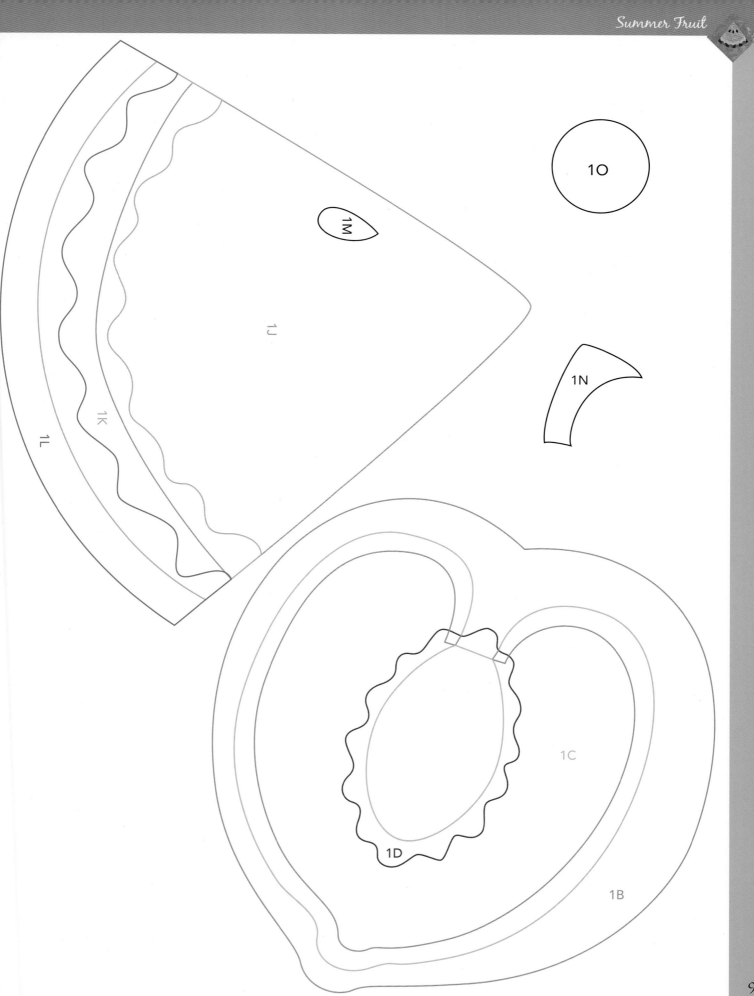

1O

1M

1J

1N

1L

1K

1C

1D

1B

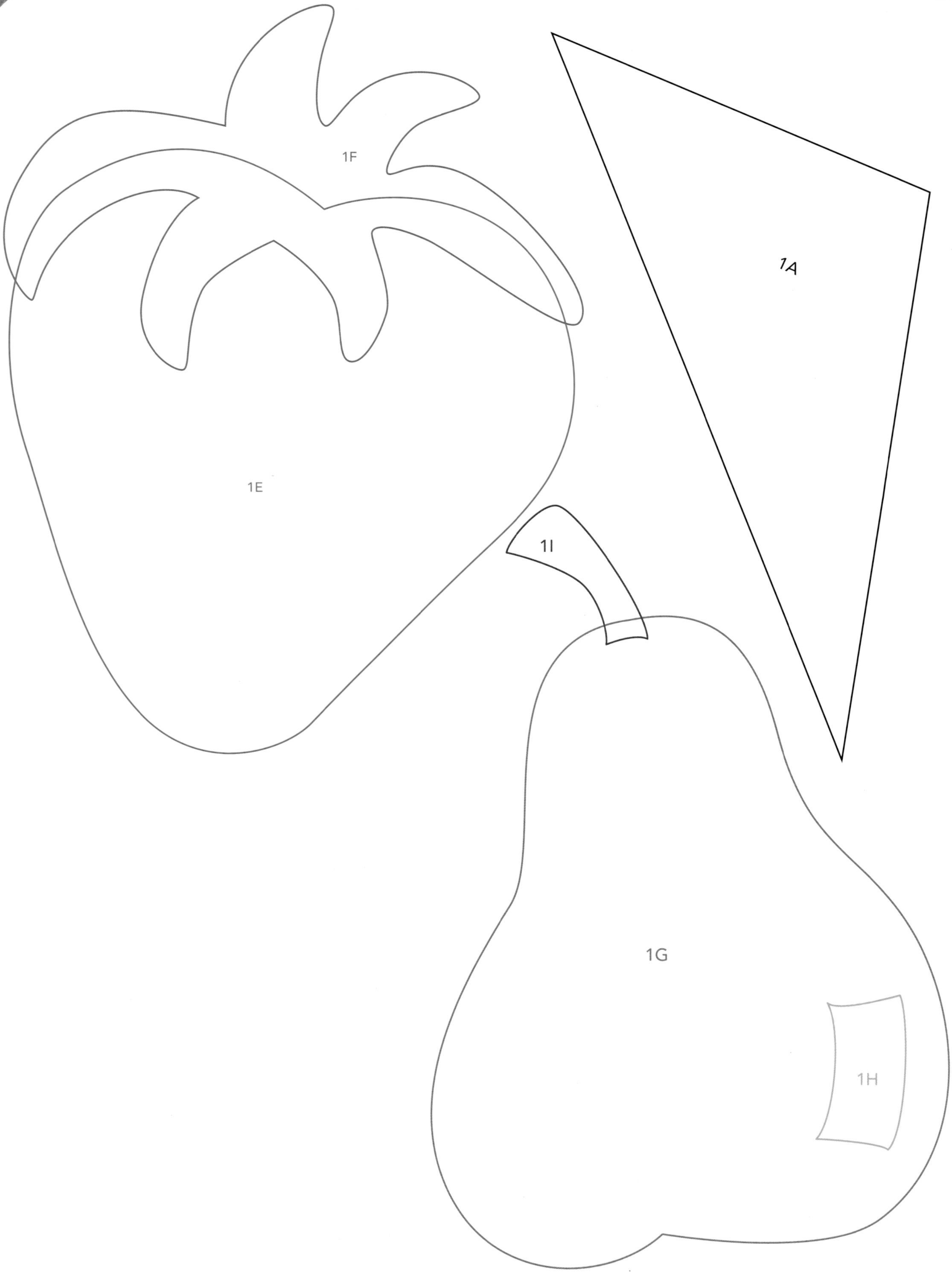

1F

1A

1E

1I

1G

1H

Big Flowers

Designed and made by Carol Burniston.
Machine quilted by Janet Murdoch.
Finished quilt: 53″ × 71″
Finished blocks: 9″ × 9″

*F*lowers for all seasons! These gorgeous flowering beauties are to be enjoyed all year 'round, so get ready to stitch your own bouquet of these *Big Flowers.* You can almost smell their sweet fragrance.

Materials You'll Need

For the Nine-Patch blocks

- ⅝ yard total assorted dark orange prints
- ⅝ yard total assorted light orange prints
- ⅝ yard total assorted dark pink prints
- ⅝ yard total assorted light pink prints
- ⅞ yard total assorted red prints
- 1¼ yards total assorted yellow prints for Nine-Patch blocks and middle border
- ⅜ yard blue print for inner border
- 1 yard red print for outer border and binding
- At least 40 large scraps of assorted colorful prints for flower appliqués
- 1¼ yards total assorted green prints for flower, stem, and leaf appliqués
- 3½ yards fabric for backing
- 61″ × 79″ piece of batting
- 8 yards lightweight 22″-wide fusible web
- Monofilament thread
- Template plastic (optional)

Cutting the Fabric

Cut strips from the crosswise grain of the fabric.

From the assorted dark orange prints, cut:

- 54 squares, 3½″ × 3½″ (Nine-Patch blocks)

From the assorted light orange prints, cut:

- 45 squares, 3½″ × 3½″ (Nine-Patch blocks)

From the assorted dark pink prints, cut:

- 45 squares, 3½″ × 3½″ (Nine-Patch blocks)

From the assorted light pink prints, cut:

- 45 squares, 3½″ × 3½″ (Nine-Patch blocks)

From the assorted red prints, cut:

- 72 squares, 3½″ × 3½″ (Nine-Patch blocks)

From the assorted yellow prints, cut:

- 54 squares, 3½″ × 3½″ (Nine-Patch blocks)
- 78 rectangles, 2½″ × 3½″ (border)

From the blue print, cut:

- 7 strips, 1½″ × 40″ (border)

From the red print, cut:

- 7 strips, 1½″ × 40″ (border)
- 7 strips, 2½″ × 40″ (binding)

Piecing the Nine-Patch Blocks

1. Lay out 9 assorted dark orange 3½″ × 3½″ squares in 3 horizontal rows. Sew the squares into rows. Press the seams in alternating directions with each row. Sew the rows together to make a Nine-Patch block. Press. Make 6.

2. Repeat Step 1 with 9 assorted light orange 3½″ × 3½″ squares. Make 5.

3. Repeat Step 1 with 9 assorted dark pink 3½″ × 3½″ squares. Make 5.

4. Repeat Step 1 with 9 assorted light pink 3½″ × 3½″ squares. Make 5.

5. Repeat Step 1 with 9 assorted red 3½″ × 3½″ squares. Make 8.

6. Repeat Step 1 with 9 assorted yellow 3½″ × 3½″ squares. Make 6.

Assembling the Quilt

Referring to the quilt photo (page 11), lay out the 35 Nine-Patch blocks in 7 horizontal rows of 5 blocks each. Sew the blocks into rows. Press the seams in alternating directions with each row. Sew the rows together. Press the seams in one direction. The quilt should now measure 45½″ × 63½″.

Cutting for Appliqué

The patterns for these appliqués are on pages 15–17. Refer to *Making Templates* (page 43).

Note: For the appliquéd flowers, you'll choose from your selection of 40 assorted colorful prints. For each flower, use a different print for each flower part. For the appliquéd *leaves and stems,* you'll choose from your selection of assorted green prints.

Flower #1: select 6 different colorful prints.
- Pattern 2A: make 12 flower petals.
- Patterns 2L, 2M, 2J, 2I, and 2P: make 1 flower part from each.
- Pattern 2T: make 1 leaf from the assorted green prints.
- Pattern 2U: make 4 stem parts from the same green print.

Flower #2: select 5 different colorful prints.
- Pattern 2B: make 10 flower petals.
- Patterns 2Q, 2R, 2O, and 2K: make 1 flower part from each.
- Pattern 2U: make 4 stem parts from the same green print.

Flower #3: select 5 different colorful prints.
- Pattern 2C: make 11 flower petals.
- Patterns 2Q, 2R, 2S, and 2K: make 1 flower part from each.
- Pattern 2U: make 4 stem parts from the same green print.

Flower #4: select 5 different colorful prints.
- Pattern 2A: make 12 flower petals.
- Patterns 2F, 2G, and 2J: make 1 flower part from each.
- Pattern 2K: make 7 flower centers.
- Pattern 2U: make 3 stem parts from the same green print.

Flower #5: select 6 different colorful prints.
- Pattern 2E: make 12 flower petals.
- Patterns 2L, 2M, 2N, 2O, and 2K: make 1 flower part from each.
- Pattern 2U: make 4 stem parts from the same green print.

Flower #6: select 6 different colorful prints.
- Pattern 2D: make 12 flower petals.
- Patterns 2F, 2G, 2H, 2I, and 2P: make 1 flower part from each.
- Pattern 2U: make 3 stem parts from the same green print.

Flower #7: select 5 different colorful prints.

- Pattern 2C: make 11 flower petals.
- Patterns 2Q, 2R, 2S, and 2K: make 1 flower part from each.
- Pattern 2U: make 4 stem parts from the same green print.

Flower #8: select 5 different colorful prints.

- Pattern 2B: make 10 flower petals.
- Patterns 2Q, 2R, 2O, and 2K: make 1 flower part from each.
- Pattern 2U: make 3 stem parts from the same green print.

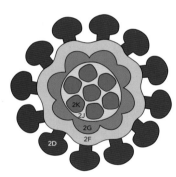

Flower #9: select 5 different colorful prints.

- Pattern 2D: make 12 flower petals.
- Patterns 2F, 2G, and 2J: make 1 flower part from each.
- Pattern 2K: make 7 flower centers.
- Pattern 2T: make 2 leaves from the same green print.
- Pattern 2U: make 2 stem parts from the same green print.

Flower #10: select 6 different colorful prints.

- Pattern 2E: make 11 flower petals.
- Patterns 2L, 2M, 2N, 2O, and 2K: make 1 flower part from each.
- Pattern 2U: make 1 stem part from a green print.

Flower #11: select 5 different colorful prints.

- Pattern 2A: make 12 flower petals.
- Patterns 2L, 2M, 2N, and 2I: make 1 flower part from each.
- Pattern 2T: make 2 leaves from the same green print.
- Pattern 2U: make 2 stem parts from the same green print.

Appliquéing the Big Flowers

Refer to *Fusible Appliqué* **(page 44).**

1. On a flat surface, layer the pieces of one flower together but don't include the flower petals yet. To keep the fabric layers from becoming too thick, use a pencil or a disappearing pen to lightly outline the upper flower pieces on the lower, larger flower pieces. Cut out the center areas of the lower pieces, leaving approximately ¼˝ of fabric inside the drawn lines. *Be sure you don't get carried away and cut into the top flower pieces, or you'll end up with a hole in your flower!*

2. Repeat Step 1 for each of the 11 flowers.

3. Now your creativity comes into play! Referring to the quilt photo (page 11), use a large flat surface such as a design wall, table, or floor to lay out the quilt and arrange all the flowers, stems, and leaves. Cut the stem parts as needed to get them to angle and bend. Overlap the stem ends slightly as you lay them out to make a complete stem.

4. Because you will be fusing and finishing the edges of the appliqués on the entire quilt instead of on one block at a time, it may be easier to pin the stems and leaves in place first and remove the flower pieces for now. Fuse the stems and leaves to the quilt. Finish the pieced ends of the stem appliqués with a narrow zigzag stitch and monofilament thread. Finish the edges of the stem and leaf appliqués with a machine blanket stitch and monofilament thread.

5. After you've finished with the leaves and stems, lay out the quilt again and place the flowers back on the stems as previously selected. Pin the flower pieces in place and then fuse them to the quilt. Finish the edges of the flower appliqués with a machine blanket stitch and monofilament thread.

Adding the Border

1. Sew the 1½″ × 40″ blue print strips end-to-end as needed and cut two 1½″ × 63½″ strips for the inner side borders and two 1½″ × 47½″ strips for the inner top and bottom borders.

2. Sew the blue 1½″ × 63½″ strips to the sides of the quilt. Press the seams toward the blue strips. Sew the blue 1½″ × 47½″ strips to the top and bottom of the quilt. Press.

3. Sew 22 yellow print 2½″ × 3½″ rectangles together end-to-end to make a middle side border. Press. Trim the ends of the strip to measure 2½″ × 65½″. Make 2.

4. Sew 17 yellow print 2½″ × 3½″ rectangles together end-to-end to make a middle top or bottom border. Press. The strip should measure 2½″ × 51½″. Make 2.

5. Sew the yellow 2½″ × 65½″ strips to the sides of the quilt. Press the seams toward the blue strips. Sew the yellow 2½″ × 51½″ strips to the top and bottom of the quilt. Press.

6. Piece the red print 1½″ × 40″ strips end-to-end as needed and cut into two 1½″ × 69½″ strips for the outer side borders and two 1½″ × 53½″ strips for the outer top and bottom borders.

7. Sew the red 1½″ × 69½″ strips to the sides of the quilt. Press the seams toward the red strips. Sew the red 1½″ × 53½″ strips to the top and bottom of the quilt. Press.

Quilting and Binding

Refer to *Basic Quiltmaking Tips* **(pages 43–47) as needed to finish your quilt.**

Divide the backing fabric in half selvage-to-selvage. Re-seam and trim to make a 61″ × 79″ backing. Layer the quilt top, batting, and backing. Baste the layers and quilt as desired. Make the binding using the 2½″-wide red strips and finish the edges of the quilt.

Appliqué Patterns

The appliqué patterns are reversed for fusible appliqué. For hand appliqué, reverse the patterns and make templates (see *Making Templates*, **page 43).**

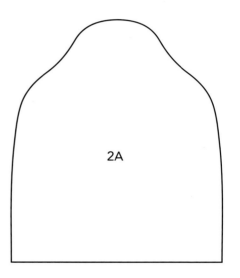

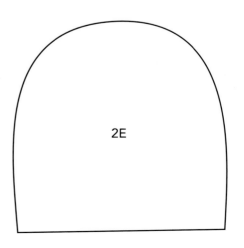

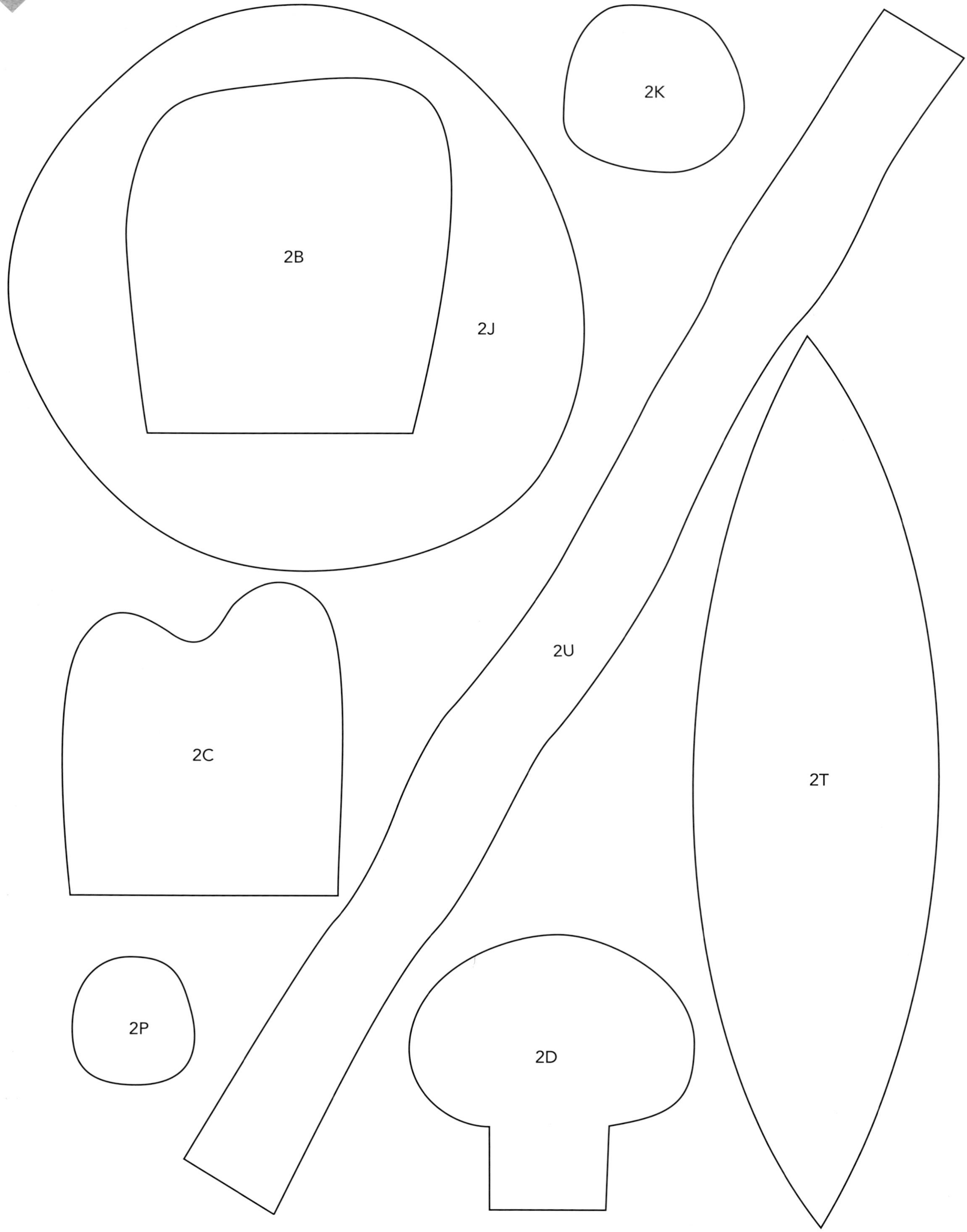

2K

2B

2J

2C

2U

2T

2P

2D

2O

2N

2M

2L

Enlarge 200%.

2S

2R

2Q

Enlarge 200%.

2I

2H

2G

2F

Enlarge 200%.

Elephants on Safari

Designed and made by Carol Burniston.
Machine quilted by Janet Murdoch.
Finished quilt: 65″ × 77″

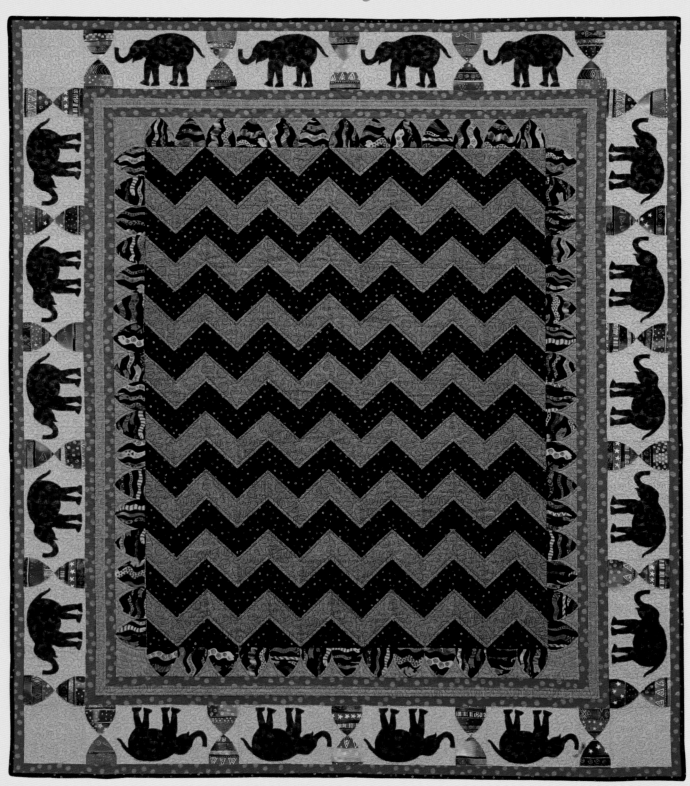

*D*reaming of an exotic excursion into the land of elephants and adventure? Create your own *Elephants on Safari* quilt as you contemplate magical days and nights in the sweeping savanna of Africa.

Materials You'll Need

- 1½ yards medium purple print for zigzag quilt center

- 2¼ yards black print for zigzag quilt center and binding

- ⅞ yard green print for hourglass triangle appliqué foundation strips and middle-border strips

- 1 yard red print for inner-, middle-, and outer-border strips

- 1¾ yards gold print for elephant and hourglass appliqué foundations

- 1 yard dark purple print for elephant appliqués

- ¾ yard multicolored print 1 for inner-border hourglass triangle appliqués

- ½ yard multicolored print 2 for Hourglass Triangle block appliqués

- 4⅜ yards fabric for backing

- 73″ × 85″ piece of batting

- 3½ yards lightweight 22″-wide fusible web

- Monofilament thread

- Template plastic (optional)

Cutting the Fabric

Cut strips from the crosswise grain of the fabric. Refer to *Tip, Preparing for Appliqué* (page 43).

From the medium purple print, cut:

- 12 strips, 3⅞″ × 40″; crosscut into:
  111 squares, 3⅞″ × 3⅞″ (zigzag quilt center)

From the black print, cut:

- 12 strips, 3⅞″ × 40″; crosscut into:
  111 squares, 3⅞″ × 3⅞″ (zigzag quilt center)

- 8 strips, 2½″ × 40″ (binding)

From the green print, cut:

- 5 strips, 3½″ × 40″ (inner-border hourglass triangle foundations)

- 6 strips, 1½″ × 40″ (middle border)

From the red print, cut:

- 19 strips, 1½″ × 40″ (inner, middle, and outer borders)

From the gold print, cut:

- 5 strips, 6½″ × 40″; crosscut into:
  4 squares, 6½″ × 6½″ (outer quilt corners)
  18 rectangles, 6½″ × 9½″ (elephant foundations)

- 4 strips, 3½″ × 40″; crosscut into:
  22 rectangles, 3½″ × 6½″ (hourglass foundations)

Piecing the Zigzag Quilt Center

1. Draw a diagonal line on the wrong side of each of the 111 purple 3⅞″ × 3⅞″ squares. Place a marked purple square right sides together with an unmarked black 3⅞″ × 3⅞″ square. Make 111.

2. Sew ¼″ away on both sides of the drawn line and then cut on the drawn line to make 2 half-square triangle units. Press each unit open with the seam toward the darker fabric. Make 221 (you'll have 1 extra unit).

3. Align 13 of the half-square triangle units to create the first row of the pattern. Sew the units together. Repeat to make a total of 17 rows.

4. Lay out the 17 rows, alternating the orientation of the black triangles from row to row to create the zigzag pattern. When the rows are sewn together, the zigzag section should measure 39½″ × 51½″.

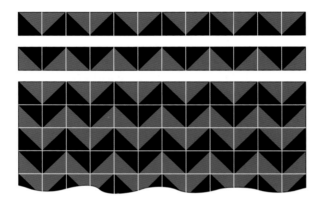

Cutting for Appliqué

The patterns for these appliqués are on pages 22–23. Refer to *Making Templates* (page 43).

For the elephants, use:

- Pattern 3A: make 18 from the dark purple print.

For the inner-border hourglass triangles, use:

- Pattern 3B: make 60 from multicolored print 1.

For the Hourglass Triangle blocks, use:

- Pattern 3B: make 44 from multicolored print 2.

Appliquéing the Elephant and Hourglass Blocks and the Hourglass Triangle Border

You will need 18 Elephant blocks, 22 Hourglass blocks, and 4 hourglass triangle border strips. Refer to *Fusible Appliqué* (page 44).

1. For the Elephant blocks, position and fuse an elephant (3A) to each gold 6½″ × 9½″ foundation rectangle. Make 18.

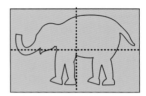

2. For the Hourglass blocks, position and fuse 2 multicolored print 2 hourglass triangles (3B) to each gold 3½″ × 6½″ foundation rectangle. Make 22.

3. For the hourglass triangle border foundations, piece together the green 3½″ × 40″ strips end-to-end as needed and cut two 3½″ × 51½″ strips for the side appliqué strips and two 3½″ × 45½″ strips for the top and bottom appliqué strips.

4. Position and fuse 17 multicolored print 1 hourglass triangles (3B) to each green 3½″ × 51½″ strip. Remember to place the appliqués ¼″ away from the strips' long edges to allow for a ¼″ seam allowance. Make 2.

5. Position and fuse 13 multicolored print 1 hourglass triangles (3B) onto each green 3½″ × 45½″ strip. Make sure the appliqués are 3½″ away from the ends of each strip and ¼″ away from the strips' long edges. Make 2.

6. Finish the edges of the appliqués with a machine blanket stitch and monofilament thread. Sew one 3½″ × 51½″ triangle-appliquéd strip to each side of the quilt. Press the seams toward the border strips. Sew the 3½″ × 45½″ triangle-appliquéd strips to the top and bottom of the quilt. Press.

Adding the Inner and Middle Borders

1. Piece together the red 1½″ × 40″ strips end-to-end as needed and cut to make:

   • 2 strips, 1½″ × 57½″, for the inner side borders

   • 2 strips, 1½″ × 47½″, for the inner top and bottom borders

   • 2 strips, 1½″ × 61½″, for the middle side borders

   • 2 strips, 1½″ × 51½″, for the middle top and bottom borders

   • 2 strips, 1½″ × 75½″, for the outer side borders

   • 2 strips, 1½″ × 65½″, for the outer top and bottom borders

2. Piece together the 1½″ × 40″ green strips end-to-end as needed and cut to make:

   • 2 strips, 1½″ × 59½″, for the middle side borders

   • 2 strips, 1½″ × 49½″, for the middle top and bottom borders

3. Sew the red 1½″ × 57½″ strips to the sides of the quilt. Press the seams toward the strips. Sew the red 1½″ × 47½″ strips to the top and bottom of the quilt. Press.

4. Sew the green 1½″ × 59½″ strips to the sides of the quilt. Press the seams toward the strips. Sew the green 1½″ × 49½″ strips to the top and bottom of the quilt. Press.

5. Sew the red 1½″ × 61½″ strips to the sides of the quilt. Press the seams toward the strips. Sew the red 1½″ × 51½″ strips to the top and bottom of the quilt. Press.

Adding the Outer Border

1. Lay out 5 Elephant blocks and 6 Hourglass blocks in a horizontal row to make the outer side border. Sew the blocks together. Press. Make 2.

2. Lay out 4 Elephant blocks, 5 Hourglass blocks, and 2 gold 6½″ × 6½″ squares in a horizontal row to make the outer top or bottom border. Sew the blocks and squares together. Press. Make 2.

6½″   6½″

3. Sew the appliquéd side borders to the quilt. Press the seams toward the red strips. Sew the appliquéd top and bottom borders to the quilt. Press.

4. Sew the red 1½″ × 75½″ strips to the sides of the quilt. Press the seams toward the strips. Sew the red 1½ × 65½″ strips to the top and bottom of the quilt. Press.

Quilting and Binding

Refer to *Basic Quiltmaking Tips* **(pages 43–47) as needed to finish your quilt.**

Divide the backing fabric in half selvage-to-selvage. Re-seam and trim to make a 73″ × 85″ backing. Layer the quilt top, batting, and backing. Baste the layers together and quilt as desired. Make binding using the 2½″-wide black strips and finish the edges of the quilt.

Appliqué Patterns

The appliqué patterns are reversed for fusible appliqué. For hand appliqué, reverse the patterns and make templates (see *Making Templates*, page 43).

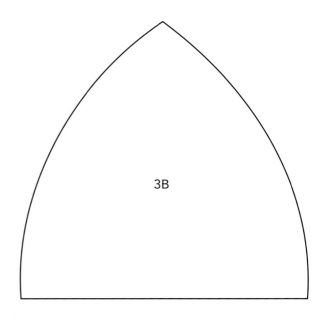

3A

Frogs and Ladybugs

Designed and made by Carol Burniston.
Machine quilted by Janet Murdoch.
Finished quilt: 48˝ × 60˝

*I*n our imaginary garden, we'll sit on a wooden bench and peer at a lily pond filled with frogs. We'll then stroll down a gravel path until we come to the fragrant rosebushes where ladybugs live. Quilts and gardens can both be wonderfully growing things!

Materials You'll Need

- 1⅜ yards total assorted blue prints for pieced background

- 2⅝ yards light orange print for pieced background and frog and ladybug appliqué foundations

- 1 yard red print for ladybug appliqués, border, and binding

- ⅜ yard green print for frog appliqués

- ¼ yard blue print for frog appliqués

- Scrap of yellow solid or subtle print for frog appliqués

- ⅛ yard black solid or subtle print for frog and ladybug appliqués

- 3⅔ yards fabric for backing

- 56″ × 68″ piece of batting

- 1¾ yards lightweight 22″-wide fusible web

- Thread to match appliqués

- Black embroidery floss

- Template plastic (optional)

Cutting the Fabric

Cut strips from the crosswise grain of the fabric. Refer to *Tip, Preparing for Appliqué* (page 43).

From the assorted blue prints, cut:

- 29 strips, 1½″ × 40″; crosscut into:
  742 squares, 1½″ × 1½″

From the light orange print, cut:

- 40 strips, 1½″ × 40″; crosscut into:
  572 squares, 1½″ × 1½″
  64 rectangles, 1½″ × 3½″
  60 rectangles, 1½″ × 5½″
  12 rectangles, 1½″ × 7½″

- 2 strips, 7½″ × 40″; crosscut into:
  9 squares, 7½″ × 7½″ (frog foundations)

- 3 strips, 3½″ × 40″; crosscut into:
  26 squares, 3½″ × 3½″ (ladybug foundations)

From the red print, cut:

- 6 strips, 2″ × 40″ (border)

- 6 strips, 2½″ × 40″ (binding)

Cutting for Appliqué

The patterns for these appliqués are on page 29. Refer to *Making Templates* (page 43).

For the Frog blocks, use:

- Pattern 4A: make 9 from the green print.

- Patterns 4B and 4C: make 9 each from the blue print.

- Pattern 4D: make 9 from the yellow scraps.

- Pattern 4E: make 9 from the black solid or print.

For the Ladybug blocks, use:

- Pattern 4F: make 26 from the black solid or print.

- Pattern 4G: make 26 from the red print.

Appliquéing the Frog and Ladybug Blocks

You will need 35 appliquéd blocks: 9 Frog blocks and 26 Ladybug blocks. Refer to *Fusible Appliqué* (page 44).

1. For the Frog blocks, position and fuse 1 each of 4A–4E to each light orange 7½″ × 7½″ foundation square. Make 9. Notice that each frog eye is looking in a different direction.

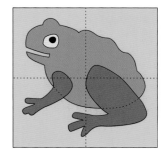

2. For the Ladybug blocks, position and fuse 1 each of 4F and 4G to each light orange 3½″ × 3½″ foundation square. Make 26.

3. Finish the edges of the appliqués with matching-colored thread and a machine blanket stitch.

4. Use 2 strands of black embroidery floss and a backstitch to embroider each ladybug's legs and antennae. For tips on embroidery, refer to *Embroidery Stitches* (page 45).

Assembling the Quilt

1. Alternating the colors, lay out 23 light orange 1½″ × 1½″ squares and 22 assorted blue 1½″ × 1½″ squares. Sew the squares into a row. Press the seams toward the blue squares. Make 6 strips and label them Row 1.

2. Referring to the diagram below, lay out 18 light orange $1\frac{1}{2}" \times 1\frac{1}{2}"$ squares, 21 assorted blue $1\frac{1}{2}" \times 1\frac{1}{2}"$ squares, and 2 light orange $1\frac{1}{2}" \times 3\frac{1}{2}"$ rectangles. Sew the squares and rectangles into a row. Press the seams toward the blue squares. Make 6 strips and label them Row 2.

3. Lay out 17 light orange $1\frac{1}{2}" \times 1\frac{1}{2}"$ squares, 18 assorted blue $1\frac{1}{2}" \times 1\frac{1}{2}"$ squares, and 2 light orange $1\frac{1}{2}" \times 5\frac{1}{2}"$ rectangles. Sew the squares and rectangles into a row. Press. Make 6 strips and label them Row 3.

4. Lay out 8 light orange $1\frac{1}{2}" \times 1\frac{1}{2}"$ squares, 14 assorted blue $1\frac{1}{2}" \times 1\frac{1}{2}"$ squares, 3 light orange $1\frac{1}{2}" \times 3\frac{1}{2}"$ rectangles, and 2 light orange $1\frac{1}{2}" \times 7\frac{1}{2}"$ rectangles. Sew the squares and rectangles into a row. Press. Make 6 strips and label them Row 4.

5. Lay out 8 light orange $1\frac{1}{2}" \times 1\frac{1}{2}"$ squares, 12 assorted blue $1\frac{1}{2}" \times 1\frac{1}{2}"$ squares, and 5 light orange $1\frac{1}{2}" \times 5\frac{1}{2}"$ rectangles. Sew the squares and rectangles into a row. Press. Make 6 and label them Row 5.

7. Lay out 5 light orange $1\frac{1}{2}" \times 1\frac{1}{2}"$ squares, 8 assorted blue $1\frac{1}{2}" \times 1\frac{1}{2}"$ squares, 1 light orange $1\frac{1}{2}" \times 3\frac{1}{2}"$ rectangle, and 1 light orange $1\frac{1}{2}" \times 5\frac{1}{2}"$ rectangle. Sew the squares and rectangles into vertical rows (columns). Press. Sew the rows together. Press. Make 18 and label them Unit 1.

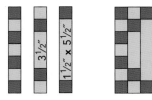

Unit 1

8. To make the Frog block, use 1 frog appliqué square and 2 Unit 1's. Sew a Unit 1 to each side of the frog appliqué square. Press. Make 9.

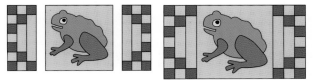

Frog block

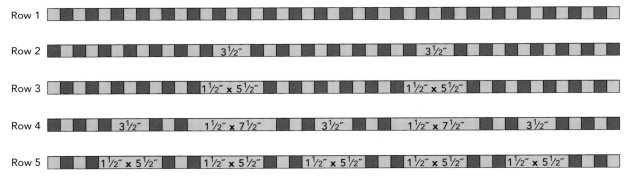

Row 1

Row 2

Row 3

Row 4

Row 5

6. Select 1 row from each of the 5 sets of rows you've just sewn. Lay the rows out in the order shown; then sew the rows together. Press the seams in one direction. Make 6 and label them Section A.

Row 1
Row 2
Row 3
Row 4
Row 5

Section A

9. Select 2 assorted blue 1½″ × 1½″ squares and 1 light orange 1½″ × 1½″ square. Sew the squares into a row. Press. Make 38 and label them Unit 2.

Unit 2

10. Select 1 ladybug square, 2 Unit 2's, and 2 light orange 1½″ × 3½″ rectangles. Sew the square, units, and rectangles together as shown. Press. Make 6 Ladybug blocks.

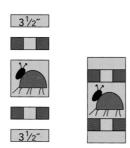

Ladybug block

11. Sew together 3 Frog blocks and 2 Ladybug blocks into a row. Press. Make 3 and label them Section B.

Section B

12. Select 2 light orange 1½″ × 3½″ rectangles, 13 Unit 2's, and 10 ladybug squares. Sew the rectangles, units, and squares into a row. Press. Make 2 and label them Section C.

1½″ × 3½″   1½″ × 3½″

Section C

13. Referring to the quilt photo (page 24) and the quilt assembly diagram (below), lay out Sections A, B, and C in 11 horizontal rows, sew them together, and press the seams in one direction.

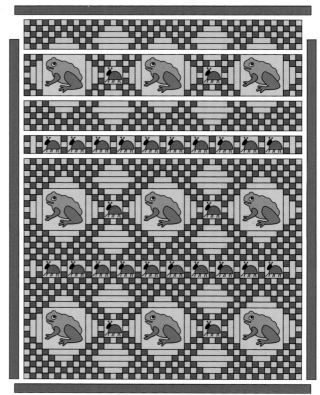

Quilt assembly diagram

Adding the Border

1. Sew together the red 2″ × 40″ strips end-to-end as necessary and cut two 2″ × 57½″ strips for the side borders and two 2″ × 48½″ strips for the top and bottom borders.

2. Sew the 2″ × 57½″ strips to the sides of the quilt. Press the seams toward the border strips. Sew the 2″ × 48½″ strips to the top and bottom of the quilt. Press.

Quilting and Binding

Refer to *Basic Quiltmaking Tips* **(pages 43–47) as needed to finish your quilt.**

Divide the backing fabric in half selvage-to-selvage. Re-seam and trim to make a 56″ × 68″ backing. Layer the quilt top, batting, and backing. Baste the layers together and quilt as desired. Make the binding using the 2½″-wide red strips and finish the edges of the quilt.

Appliqué Patterns

The appliqué patterns are reversed for fusible appliqué. For hand appliqué, reverse the patterns and make templates (see *Making Templates*, **page 43).**

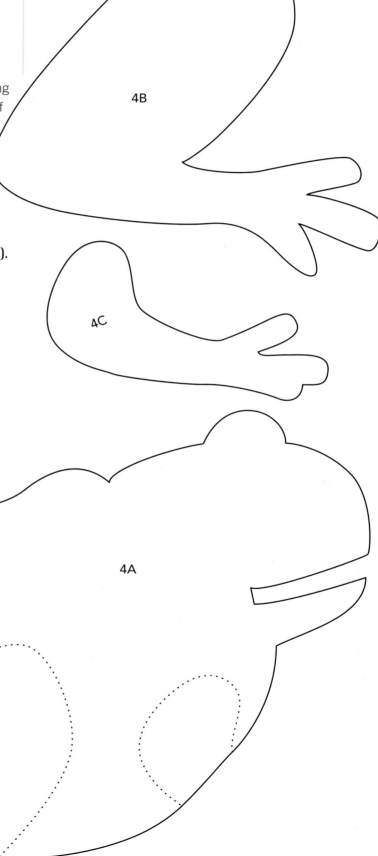

4B

4C

4G

4D

4F

4E

4A

Boxes in Boxes

Designed and made by Carol Burniston.
Machine quilted by Janet Murdoch.
Finished quilt: 56˝ × 64˝
Finished blocks: 8˝ × 8˝

Pinwheel blocks and borders spin through this quilt to create a choreographic kaleidoscope of movement. Half-square triangles and simple rectangles make this pieced quilt surprisingly fast and easy to make.

Materials You'll Need

- ¾ yard dark gray print for Pinwheel blocks
- 1⅞ yards off-white print for Pinwheel blocks, Hourglass blocks, and pinwheel border
- ⅞ yards blue print for Pinwheel blocks and binding
- 2½ yards red print for Pinwheel blocks, Hourglass blocks, and pinwheel border
- 3¾ yards fabric for backing
- 64″ × 72″ piece of batting

Cutting the Fabric

Cut strips from the crosswise grain of the fabric.

From the dark gray print, cut:

- 13 strips, 1½″ × 40″; crosscut into:
  30 rectangles, 1½″ × 6½″ (Pinwheel blocks)
  30 rectangles, 1½″ × 8½″ (Pinwheel blocks)

From the off-white print, cut:

- 9 strips, 1½″ × 40″; crosscut into:
  30 rectangles, 1½″ × 4½″ (Pinwheel blocks)
  30 rectangles, 1½″ × 6½″ (Pinwheel blocks)

- 8 squares, 9½″ × 9½″; cut in half diagonally in both directions to make 32 quarter-square triangles (Hourglass blocks). You will have 2 leftover triangles.

- 8 strips, 2⅞″ × 40″; crosscut into:
  104 squares, 2⅞″ × 2⅞″ (pinwheel border)

From the blue print, cut:

- 3 strips, 2⅞″ × 40″; crosscut into:
  30 squares, 2⅞″ × 2⅞″ (Pinwheel blocks)

- 7 strips, 2½″ × 40″ (binding)

From the red print, cut:

- 11 strips, 2⅞″ × 40″; crosscut into:
  134 squares, 2⅞″ × 2⅞″ (Pinwheel blocks and pinwheel border)

- 11 strips, 2½″ × 40″ (inner and outer borders)

- 8 squares, 9½″ × 9½″; cut in half diagonally in both directions to make 32 quarter-square triangles (Hourglass blocks). You will have 2 leftover triangles.

Piecing the Pinwheel and Hourglass Blocks

You will need a total of 30 blocks: 15 Pinwheel blocks and 15 Hourglass blocks.

Pinwheel Blocks

1. Draw a diagonal line on the wrong side of each of the 30 blue 2⅞″ × 2⅞″ squares. Place a marked blue square right sides together with an unmarked red 2⅞″ × 2⅞″ square. Make 30.

2. Sew ¼″ away on both sides of the drawn line and then cut on the drawn line to make 2 half-square triangle units. Press each unit open with the seam toward the darker fabric. Make 60.

3. Combine 4 half-square triangle units to make a pinwheel unit. Press. Make 15.

4. Sew a 1½″ × 4½″ off-white rectangle to opposite sides of each pinwheel unit. Press the seams toward the strips. Sew a 1½″ × 6½″ off-white rectangle to the top and bottom of each pinwheel unit. Press. Make 15.

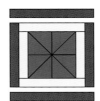

5. Sew a 1½″ × 6½″ gray rectangle to opposite sides of each pinwheel unit. Press the seams toward the gray strips. Sew a 1½″ × 8½″ gray rectangle to the top and bottom of each Pinwheel block. Press. Make 15.

Hourglass Blocks

1. Place an off-white quarter-square triangle right sides together with a red quarter-square triangle. Sew the triangles together to make a triangle pair. Press each unit open with the seam toward the darker fabric. Make 30.

2. Arrange and sew 2 triangle pairs together to make an Hourglass block. Press. Trim each Hourglass block to measure 8½″ × 8½″ square. Make 15.

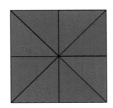

Assembling the Quilt

1. Referring to the quilt photo (page 30) and the quilt assembly diagram (page 33), lay out 15 Pinwheel blocks and 15 Hourglass blocks in horizontal rows.

2. Sew the blocks into rows. Press. Sew the rows together. Press the seams in one direction.

Piecing the Pinwheel Border

1. Using the 2⅞″ × 2⅞″ off-white squares and the remaining 2⅞″ × 2⅞″ red squares, repeat Steps 1 and 2 from the Pinwheel block instructions to make 104 half-square triangle units.

2. Using 4 of the half-square triangle units, arrange and sew a pinwheel unit. Press. Make 52.

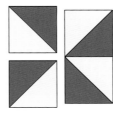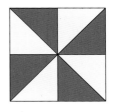

3. Referring to the quilt assembly diagram, lay out and sew 13 pinwheel units in a row to make a pinwheel border strip. Press. Make 4.

Adding the Pinwheel Border

1. Piece together and subcut the red 2½″ × 40″ strips into:

   - 2 strips, 2½″ × 48½″, for the inner side borders

   - 2 strips, 2½″ × 44½″, for the inner top and bottom borders

   - 2 strips, 2½″ × 60½″, for the outer side borders

   - 2 strips, 2½″ × 56½″, for the outer top and bottom borders

2. Sew the red 2½″ × 48½″ strips to the sides of the quilt. Press the seams toward the border strips. Sew the red 2½″ × 44½″ strips to the top and bottom of the quilt. Press.

3. Sew 2 pinwheel border strips to the sides of the quilt. Press the seams toward the border strips. Sew 2 pinwheel border strips to the top and bottom of the quilt. Press.

4. Sew the red 2½″ × 60½″ strips to the sides of the quilt. Press the seams toward the newly added border strips. Sew the red 2½″ × 56½″ strips to the top and bottom of the quilt. Press.

Quilt assembly diagram

Quilting and Binding

Refer to *Basic Quiltmaking Tips* **(pages 43–47) as needed to finish your quilt.**

Divide the backing fabric in half selvage-to-selvage. Re-seam and trim to make a 64″ × 72″ backing. Layer the quilt top, batting, and backing. Baste the layers and quilt as desired. Make the binding using the 2½″-wide blue strips and finish the edges of the quilt.

Ice Skates

Designed and made by Carol Burniston.
Machine quilted by Janet Murdoch.
Finished quilt: 55˝ × 64˝
Finished blocks: 9˝ × 9˝

*T*he snow is falling, and the ice rink is calling. Snuggle up with this quilt and keep the shivers away.

Materials You'll Need

- 3⅛ yards light blue print for ice skate appliqués, Snowflake blocks, and border
- 2¼ yards red print for Snowflake blocks, border, and binding
- ⅝ yard yellow print for ice skate appliqués
- ½ yard subtle black print for ice skate appliqués
- 3⅝ yards fabric for backing
- 63″ × 72″ piece of batting
- 2 yards lightweight 22″-wide fusible web
- Monofilament thread
- Template plastic (optional)

Cutting the Fabric

Cut strips from the crosswise grain of the fabric. Refer to *Tip, Preparing for Appliqué* (page 43).

From the light blue print, cut:

- 4 strips, 9½″ × 40″; crosscut into:
  15 squares, 9½″ × 9½″ (ice skate foundations)
- 4 strips, 2⅜″ × 40″; crosscut into:
  60 squares, 2⅜″ × 2⅜″ (Snowflake blocks)
- 3 strips, 3⅞″ × 40″; crosscut into:
  30 squares, 3⅞″ × 3⅞″ (Snowflake blocks)
- 9 strips, 2″ × 40″; crosscut into:
  90 rectangles, 2″ × 3½″ (Snowflake blocks)
- 12 strips, 2″ × 40″ (border)

From the red print, cut:

- 4 strips, 2⅜″ × 40″; crosscut into:
  60 squares, 2⅜″ × 2⅜″ (Snowflake blocks)
- 3 strips, 3⅞″ × 40″; crosscut into:
  30 squares, 3⅞″ × 3⅞″ (Snowflake blocks)

- 9 strips, 2″ × 40″; crosscut into:
  180 squares, 2″ × 2″ (Snowflake blocks)
- 12 strips, 1½″ × 40″ (border)
- 7 strips, 2½″ × 40″ (binding)

Cutting for Appliqué

The patterns for these appliqués are on page 38. Refer to *Making Templates* (page 43).

For the ice skates, use:

- Pattern 5A: make 15 from the yellow print.
- Pattern 5B: make 15 from the black print.
- Pattern 5C: make 15 from the black print.
- Pattern 5D: make 45 from the black print.

Appliquéing the Ice Skate Blocks

You will need 15 appliquéd blocks. Refer to *Fusible Appliqué* (page 44).

1. For the Ice Skate blocks, position and fuse one 5A, one 5B, one 5C, and three 5D pieces onto each 9½″ × 9½″ light blue foundation square. Make 15.

2. Finish the edges of the appliqués with a machine blanket stitch and monofilament thread.

Piecing the Snowflake Blocks

Half-Square Triangle Units

1. Draw a diagonal line on the wrong side of each of the 60 light blue 2⅜″ × 2⅜″ squares. Place a marked light blue square right sides together with an unmarked red 2⅜″ × 2⅜″ square. Make 60.

2. Sew ¼″ away on both sides of the drawn line and then cut on the drawn line to make 2 half-square triangle units. Press each unit open with the seam toward the darker fabric. Make 120.

3. Repeat Steps 1 and 2 for the larger half-square triangles but use 30 light blue 3⅞″ × 3⅞″ squares and 30 red 3⅞″ × 3⅞″ squares. Make 60.

Flying Geese Units

1. Draw a diagonal line on the wrong side of each of the 180 red 2″ × 2″ squares. Align a marked square right sides together with one end of a light blue 2″ × 3½″ rectangle. Sew on the drawn line. Trim the excess fabric, leaving a ¼″ seam allowance. Press each unit open. Make 90.

2. Align a second marked red square with the opposite end of the rectangle unit from Step 1, sew on the drawn line, trim the seam allowance to ¼″, and press to make a Flying Geese unit. Make 90.

3. Arrange and sew together 8 small half-square triangle units, 4 large half-square triangle units, and 6 Flying Geese units to make a Snowflake block. Press. Make 15.

Assembling the Quilt

1. Referring to the quilt photo (page 34) and the quilt assembly diagram (below), lay out 15 Ice Skate blocks and 15 Snowflake blocks in 6 horizontal rows.

2. Sew the blocks into rows. Press. Sew the rows together. Press the seams in one direction.

Quilt assembly diagram

Adding the Border

1. Piece together the light blue 2″ × 40″ strips end-to-end as needed and cut to make:

   - 2 strips, 2″ × 54½″, for the inner border side strips
   - 2 strips, 2″ × 48½″, for the inner border top and bottom strips
   - 2 strips, 2″ × 59½″, for the outer border side strips
   - 2 strips, 2″ × 53½″, for the outer border top and bottom strips

2. Piece together the red 1½″ × 40″ strips end-to-end as needed and cut to make:

   - 2 strips, 1½″ × 57½″, for the inner border side strips
   - 2 strips, 1½″ × 50½″, for the inner top and bottom strips
   - 2 strips, 1½″ × 62½″, for the outer border side strips
   - 2 strips, 1½″ × 55½″, for the outer border top and bottom strips

3. Sew the light blue 2″ × 54½″ strips to the sides of the quilt. Press the seams toward the border strips. Sew the light blue 2″ × 48½″ strips to the top and bottom of the quilt. Press.

4. Sew the red 1½″ × 57½″ strips to the sides of the quilt. Press the seams toward the red strips. Sew the red 1½″ × 50½″ strips to the top and bottom of the quilt. Press.

5. Sew the light blue 2″ × 59½″ strips to the sides of the quilt. Press the seams toward the red strips. Sew the light blue 2″ × 53½″ strips to the top and bottom of the quilt. Press.

6. Sew the red 1½″ × 62½″ strips to the sides of the quilt. Press the seams toward the red strips. Sew the red 1½″ × 55½″ strips to the top and bottom of the quilt. Press.

Quilting and Binding

Refer to *Basic Quiltmaking Tips* (pages 43–47) as needed to finish your quilt.

Divide the backing fabric in half selvage-to-selvage. Re-seam and trim to make a 63″ × 72″ backing. Layer the quilt top, batting, and backing. Baste the layers together and quilt as desired. Make the binding using the 2½″-wide red strips and finish the edges of the quilt.

Appliqué Patterns

The appliqué patterns are reversed for fusible appliqué. For hand appliqué, reverse the patterns and make templates (see *Making Templates*, page 43).

5C

5D

5A

5B

Stella the Dog

Designed and made by Carol Burniston.
Machine quilted by Janet Murdoch.
Finished quilt: 58″ × 71″
Finished blocks: 11″ × 11″

*P*uppy love! The puppy in this easy-to-make appliquéd quilt looks ready to fetch a Frisbee or enjoy a doggie treat. Stitch your way to puppy love.

Materials You'll Need

- 3½ yards subtle black print for Dog blocks, appliqués, and border
- 2 yards total of scraps and ⅛ yard pieces of assorted dotted prints and striped prints for sashing strips
- ⅝ yard yellow print for binding
- 1⅝ yards large dotted print for dog appliqués
- 3¾ yards backing fabric
- 66˝ × 79˝ piece of batting
- 4¼ yards lightweight 22˝-wide fusible web
- Black embroidery floss
- Monofilament thread
- Template plastic (optional)

Cutting the Fabric

Cut strips from the crosswise grain of the fabric. Refer to *Tip, Preparing for Appliqué* (page 43).

From the black print, cut:

- 7 strips, 11½˝ × 40˝; crosscut into: 20 squares, 11½˝ × 11½˝ (Dog blocks)
- 6 strips, 2½˝ × 40˝; crosscut into: 18 rectangles, 2½˝ × 11½˝ (border)

From the assorted dotted prints and striped prints, cut:

- 98 rectangles, 1½˝ × 11½˝ (sashing)
- 112 rectangles, 1½˝ × 2½˝ (sashing)

From the yellow print, cut:

- 7 strips, 2½˝ × 40˝ (binding)

Cutting for Appliqué

The patterns for these appliqués are on page 42. Refer to *Making Templates* (page 43).

For the Dog blocks, use:

- Pattern 6A: make 20 from the large dotted print.
- Pattern 6B: make 20 from the large dotted print.
- Pattern 6C: make 20 from the black print.
- Pattern 6D: make 40 from the black print.
- Pattern 6E: make 98 from the black print.

Appliquéing the Dog Blocks and Sashing Strips

You will need 20 appliquéd blocks. Refer to *Fusible Appliqué* (page 44).

1. For the Dog block, position and fuse one 6A, one 6B, one 6C, and two 6D dog parts onto each black 11½˝ × 11½˝ foundation square. Make 20.

2. For the appliquéd sashing pieces, position and fuse a 6E triangle strip ¾˝ from the right edge of each 1½˝ × 11½˝ sashing piece. Make 98 sashing pieces.

3. Finish the edges of the appliqués with a machine blanket stitch and monofilament thread.

4. Use 3 strands of black embroidery floss to back-stitch along the edges where the dog's ear and nose overlap the body. For tips on embroidery, refer to *Embroidery Stitches* (page 45).

Assembling the Quilt

1. Lay out 14 assorted print $1\frac{1}{2}'' \times 2\frac{1}{2}''$ rectangles and 4 black $2\frac{1}{2}'' \times 11\frac{1}{2}''$ rectangles in a horizontal row. Sew the rectangles together to make a top or bottom strip. Press. Make 2.

2. Lay out 14 assorted print $1\frac{1}{2}'' \times 2\frac{1}{2}''$ rectangles and 8 appliquéd $1\frac{1}{2}'' \times 11\frac{1}{2}''$ sashing pieces. Note the orientation of the triangle appliqués. Sew the sashing pieces together and press. Sew the rectangles together and press. Sew the rectangle units to the sashing pieces to complete the sashing strip. Press. Make 6.

3. Position 4 Dog blocks, 10 appliquéd sashing pieces, and 2 black $2\frac{1}{2}'' \times 11\frac{1}{2}''$ rectangles in a horizontal row. Note the orientation of the triangle appliqués. Sew the blocks and rectangles together to make a row of Dog blocks. Press. Make 5.

4. Lay out the 5 rows of Dog blocks, 6 sashing strips, and 2 top and bottom strips. Sew the rows and strips together. Press the seams toward the Dog blocks.

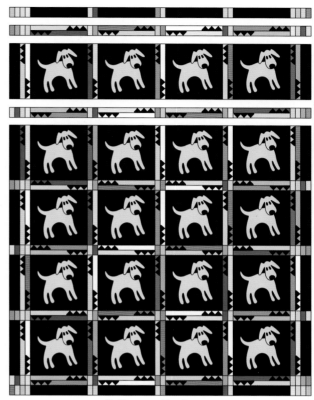

Quilt assembly diagram

Quilting and Binding

Refer to *Basic Quiltmaking Tips* (pages 43–47) as needed to finish your quilt.

Divide the backing fabric in half selvage-to-selvage. Re-seam and trim to make a 66″ × 79″ backing. Layer the quilt top, batting, and backing. Baste the layers together and quilt as desired. Make the binding using the $2\frac{1}{2}''$-wide yellow strips and finish the edges of the quilt.

Appliqué Patterns

The appliqué patterns are reversed for fusible appliqué. For hand appliqué, reverse the patterns and make templates (see *Making Templates*, page 43).

6A

6B

6C

6D

6E

Basic Quiltmaking Tips

The following pages contain the basic information you need to complete the quilts in this book, as well as many other quilt projects you may choose to make. *Yardages are based on 40″-wide fabric.*

Machine Piecing and Pressing

Use a ¼″ seam allowance for all piecing.

In general, press seams toward the darker fabric or in the direction that creates the least bulk. Unless instructed otherwise, when sewing blocks into rows, press the seams in odd-numbered rows in one direction and press the seams in even-numbered rows in the opposite direction. This practice creates opposing (or nesting) seams. Opposing seams are easier to match, and reduce bulkiness when the rows are joined.

Preparing for Appliqué

TIP Machine blanket stitching around appliqués can cause the background block to shrink or become distorted. You may want to cut the background blocks ½″ larger than stated in the instructions. For example, if the instructions call for background blocks to be 9½″ × 9½″, cut the blocks 10″ × 10″. After the appliqués have been fused in place and the edges finished with machine blanket stitching, trim the block to the size stated in the instructions.

Lightly press each background block in half vertically and horizontally to find the center of the block and to create placement guidelines for the appliqués. Press carefully so you don't stretch the block.

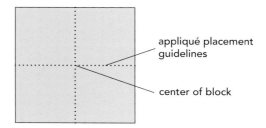

appliqué placement guidelines

center of block

Making Templates

Most of the quilt designs in this book include full-size pattern pieces that you may want to cut using templates. Look for clear, easy-to-cut template plastic at quilt shops or use your favorite mail-order sources.

To make a template, place the plastic over each pattern and trace with a fine-point permanent marker. *Do not add seam allowances; cut out the template directly on the drawn lines.*

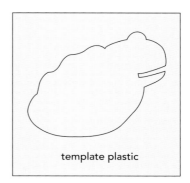

template plastic

TIP An alternative to templates is to photo-copy pattern pieces onto plain copy paper. After I make copies of the pattern pieces, I use a small, inexpensive lightbox to trace the pattern pieces onto the paper side of lightweight fusible web.

Fusible Appliqué

The appliqué patterns in this book are *reversed* for fusible appliqué. You can find fusible web at quilt and sewing shops. Be sure to get the lightweight fusible web. Instructions for these products vary by manufacturer, so read the product instructions before you begin.

You will find one or more appliqué placement diagrams with most projects to guide you in placing the appliqués. Each pattern piece is identified by a unique letter.

1. Place the fusible web paper-side-up over the pattern pieces or place the cut-out template on the paper side of the fusible web. Use a pencil to trace the required number of each pattern piece onto the fusible web. Be sure to space the pieces at least ½˝ apart. Cut out the pieces ¼˝ outside the traced lines.

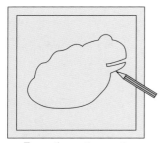 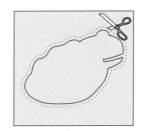

Trace the pattern onto the fusible web.

Cut out ¼˝ outside the line.

2. Fusible web can make medium and large appliqués too stiff. To prevent this, after tracing the pattern to the fusible web, cut out the center of the paper shape, leaving approximately ½˝ of paper and web inside the drawn line. This technique will leave fusible web around the edges of the appliqué but eliminate stiffness in the center.

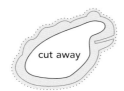

cut away

Cut out the center of the paper shape.

3. Follow the manufacturer's instructions to press the adhesive side of the fusible web to the wrong side of the appropriate appliqué fabrics. Allow to cool. Cut out the fabric shapes directly on the traced lines. Peel off the paper backing.

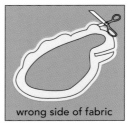

wrong side of fabric

Cut directly on the drawn line.

4. Refer to the quilt photo or the appliqué placement diagram in the project instructions to arrange the fabric pieces on the appliqué background.

 Use an Appliqué Overlay as a Placement Guide.

An overlay is a drawing of the finished block on a clear piece of plastic that you place over your background block to help you position the appliqués. Quilter's Vinyl from C&T Publishing can be found at any fabric store and works very well for this. Alternatively, you can use a simple sheet protector with the edges cut away.

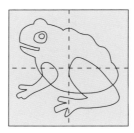

On a photocopier, enlarge the placement diagram to the actual size of the block. Lay the plastic over the drawing of an appliqué placement diagram and trace the drawing with a permanent, fine-point marker. Include the dashed lines.

5. Follow the manufacturer's instructions to fuse the appliqués to the background.

6. Use .004-weight monofilament nylon thread as the top thread in your sewing machine to finish the raw edges of the appliqués with a machine blanket stitch. This invisible thread saves

blanket stitch

time. You don't need to constantly change thread color to match the appliqués and the thread can hide imperfections in stitching. Be sure to adjust the machine tension so the bottom thread is not visible on top. You may need to loosen the top tension slightly. You can certainly use matching-colored threads if you prefer.

Hand Appliqué

If you prefer to hand stitch rather than fuse the appliqués, *reverse the appliqué patterns* and make templates as described on page 43.

1. Place the template of the reversed pattern right side up on the right side of the appropriate appliqué fabric. Trace the template onto the fabric using a pencil or an erasable fabric marker of your choice. Cut out the fabric shape, adding a ¼″ turn-under allowance.

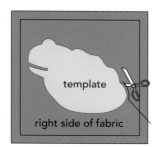

Add a ¼″ turn-under allowance to cut shapes.

2. Refer to the quilt photo or appliqué placement diagram in the project instructions to arrange the fabric pieces on the appliqué background. Fold under the fabric on the drawn line as you appliqué the shapes to the background, using a single strand of matching-colored thread and a blind or hem stitch.

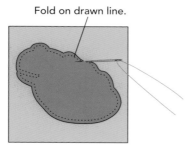

Fold on drawn line.

Match thread to color of appliqué.

Embroidery Stitches

Two of the quilts in this book, *Frogs and Ladybugs* and *Stella the Dog,* feature embroidered details. Refer to the following diagram to create the embroidery stitch used in these quilts.

Backstitch

Adding the Borders

To avoid wavy borders, cut border strips to fit the quilt. Border measurements are included in the instructions for every project, but quilts don't always come out exactly the size they're supposed to (especially large quilts).

1. Measure the quilt top through the center from top to bottom. Cut 2 border strips to that length, piecing them if necessary. Pin the strips to the sides of the quilt top, with right sides together. Match the centers and ends of the strips to the center and ends of the quilt top, easing if necessary. Sew the border strips to the sides of the quilt top with ¼″ seam allowances. Press as instructed, usually toward the border strips.

2. Measure the quilt through the center from side to side, including the borders you've just added. Repeat Step 1 to cut, pin, and sew the strips to the top and bottom of the quilt. Press.

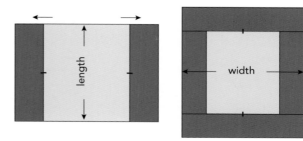

length

width

Preparing the Quilt Backing

The backing fabric needs to be at least 4″ larger than the quilt top on all sides. In most cases, you will need to seam the backing to have a large enough piece. Prewash the fabric and remove the selvages before dividing and piecing the backing fabric. To economize, you can piece the backing with vertical or horizontal seams, and you can also include any fabric or blocks in your collection.

Vertical seam   Horizontal seam

Marking the Quilting Design

If you plan to stitch in-the-ditch or outline quilt a uniform distance from the seamlines, marking the quilting pattern on your quilt top is probably unnecessary. However, for more complex quilting designs, you'll want to mark the quilt top before assembling the layers. To be sure you can erase or wash out the marks, test your fabric marker on a swatch.

Batting

You have many batting choices. Polyester and cotton battings are the most popular. I prefer cotton battings for my quilts. Cotton battings are flat and easy to quilt, and they help wall quilts to hang well.

You can purchase batting either prepackaged or by the yard. Whichever you choose, you will want the batting to be at least 4″ larger than your quilt top on all sides.

Basting the Quilt

If you plan to machine quilt, pin baste the quilt layers together with safety pins placed approximately 6″ apart. Begin in the center and pin toward the edges, first in vertical rows and then in horizontal rows to form a grid. If you plan to hand quilt, baste the layers together using a long needle and a single knotted strand of contrasting-colored thread. Begin in the center and stitch toward the edges, first in vertical rows and then in horizontal rows to form a grid. Lines of basting should be no more than 4″ apart. Finish by basting around the outside edges of the quilt.

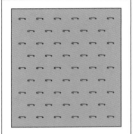 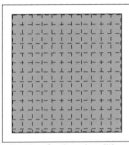

Basting for machine   Basting for hand quilting
quilting

Quilting

All of the quilts in this book are quilted by machine, and I highly recommend machine quilting. It takes much less time than hand quilting, and that means you can start another quilt much sooner.

Whether you quilt your quilts or have someone do it for you, there are many ways to quilt and many designs to choose from. You can use regular quilting thread in colors that blend or decorative threads that enhance the colorful combinations in the quilt designs.

Quilting in-the-ditch   Outline quilting

When you've finished the quilting, use a ruler and rotary cutter to trim the backing and batting even with the quilt top.

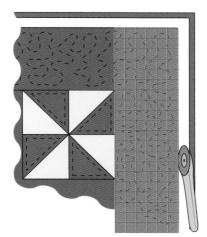

Trim the quilt's edges.

Binding

I cut my binding strips 2½″ wide on the straight grain of the fabric. The instructions for each quilt tell you the number of strips you'll need to cut.

1. Sew the strips together end-to-end to make a continuous binding strip. Press the seams open and then press the entire strip in half lengthwise, with wrong sides together.

2. Align the raw edges of the binding with the raw edges of the quilt top. Starting a few inches from the beginning of the strip and near the middle of one of the sides of the quilt, stitch the binding to the quilt through all layers with a ¼″ seam allowance.

3. Stop sewing with a backstitch ¼″ from the first corner. Lift the presser foot and needle. Rotate the quilt one-quarter turn. Fold the binding so it extends straight above the quilt and then fold down the binding even with the raw edge of the next side of the quilt top. Resume sewing at the folded edge, mitering each corner in this way as you come to it. Stop stitching approximately 4″ from the starting end of the binding.

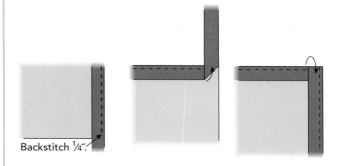

Backstitch ¼″.

4. To finish the binding, unfold the starting end of the strip and turn the fabric under ¼″ to create a finished edge. Refold the strip. Lay the end of the binding over the folded starting end, with the raw edges even with the edge of the quilt. Finish stitching the binding to the quilt top with a ¼″ seam allowance and trim the excess binding strip, leaving an overlap of approximately ½″.

5. Fold the binding strip over the raw edge of the quilt to the quilt back, covering the machine stitching. Hand stitch the binding to the quilt with matching-colored thread, mitering the corners.

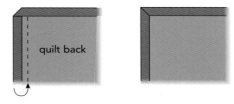

quilt back

About the Author

Photo by Cassie Burniston

Carol Burniston has been quilting for a few years and sewing forever; she claims to have been born with the love-of-fabric gene. While she was growing up with five sisters and one brother, there was always one room in the house called "the sewing room." The sewing room was where the action took place. It was where Carol and her sisters congregated with their mother to share stories and to learn how to sew. Carol and her sisters quickly went from sewing straight lines on striped fabric to sewing their own clothes and piecing quilts with left-over fabric scraps.

Today, Carol enjoys using bright, fun colors in her quilts. When she walks into a fabric store, she is drawn to the colorful fabrics; they make her smile. She enjoys using contrasting colors, combining them to create playful, light-hearted designs.

Carol's sisters, Barbara Brandeburg and Teri Christopherson, have been successful book authors for a number of years. Another of Carol's sisters, Janet Murdock, an award-winning longarm quilter, machine quilted all the projects for this, Carol's second book with C&T Publishing.

Resources

For a list of other fine books from C&T Publishing, ask for a free catalog:

C&T Publishing, Inc.
P.O. Box 1456
Lafayette, CA 94549
(800) 284-1114
Email: **ctinfo@ctpub.com**
Website: **www.ctpub.com**

For quilting supplies:

Cotton Patch
1025 Brown Ave.
Lafayette, CA 94549
(800) 835-4418
(925) 283-7883
Email: **CottonPa@aol.com**
Website: **www.quiltusa.com**

NOTE: Fabrics used in the quilts shown may not be currently available as fabric manufacturers keep most fabrics in print for only a short time.

C&T Publishing's professional photography services are now available to the public.
Visit us at **www.ctmediaservices.com**